The Ultin

Unofficial

Chelsea

Quiz Book

601 Fun Questions for Blues

Fans Everywhere

By

David Lynam

For Chelsea fans everywhere...

"Before my mother died, she told me not to leave Chelsea" – Frank Lampard

"The way of the manager leaving the club by deciding to walk away, no chance! I will never do this to Chelsea supporters" – Jose Mourinho

"I still say if the ball is there to be won I will go for it, whether with my head or whatever, and if it means us scoring or stopping a goal, I won't think twice" – John Terry

"I believe a lot in destiny and I think that if something didn't happen it was for a reason" – Didier Drogba

# # #

Welcome to the ultimate Chelsea quiz book.

In this book you are going to find 601 questions about Chelsea, split into thirty separate rounds. You have the chance to test your knowledge and memory, and the questions cover a wide range of topics, including key matches, big transfers, past and present players, club history, and managers of the blues.

The rounds are not split into themes, meaning that each round provides a random mix of trivia to test your knowledge. There is also a mix of difficulty, so this book will really see how much of a Chelsea buff you really are. The book is interesting and informative, and will provide hours of fun for the most passionate Chelsea fans everywhere.

Good luck...

Table of Contents

# # #

Round 1

1. By how many points did Chelsea win the 2004-2005 Premier League title?

2. Adrian Mutu was signed from which club?

3. Against which team did Gordon Durie score five goals in a famous 1989 league match?

4. Albert Ferrer, who played for Chelsea in the 2000s, was what nationality?

5. Allan Harris wore which shirt number in the 1967 FA Cup Final?

6. Andre Villas Boas was appointed Chelsea manager in which year?

7. Andreas Christensen was loaned to which team for the 2016-2017 season?

8. Andrew Wilson became Chelsea's most expensive player in which year?

9. Andrew Wilson was once Chelsea's record singing. How much did he cost?

10. Andy Myers left Chelsea in which season?

11. Ashley Cole joined Chelsea in which year?

12. Asmir Begovic wore which shirt number for Chelsea during the 2016-2017 season?

13. At which stadium did Chelsea beat Watford 5-1 in the 1970 FA

Cup Semi Final?

14. Avram Grant was appointed as Chelsea manager in which year?

15. Baba Rahman was loaned to which team for the 2016-2017 season?

16. Bob McRoberts became Chelsea's most expensive player in which year?

17. Bob McRoberts was once Chelsea's record singing. How much did he cost?

18. Bob Turnbull was the top scorer for Chelsea in which season?

19. Bobby Gould took charge of Chelsea in the 1980s for how many games?

20. Bobby Tambling wore which shirt number in the 1967 FA Cup Final?

Answers

1. 12

2. Parma

3. Walsall

4. Spanish

5. 2

6. 2011

7. Borussia Mönhengladbach

8. 1923

9. £6,500

10. 1999-2000

11. 2014

12. 1

13. White Hart Lane

14. 2007

15. Schalke 04

16. 1905

17. £100

18. 1926-27

19. 2

20. 10

Round 2

1. Bobby Tambling made his Chelsea debut in what decade?

2. Bobby Tambling was the top scorer for Chelsea in which season?

3. Branislav Ivanovic is from which country?

4. By what score did Chelsea beat Real Madrid in the 1998 UEFA Super Cup?

5. Carlo Ancelotti won the Premier League with Chelsea on how many occasions?

6. Carlo Cudicini signed for Chelsea in which year?

7. Carlo Cudicini signed for Chelsea during which season?

8. Celestine Babayaro, who played for Chelsea in the 2000s, was what nationality?

9. Cesc Fabregas wore which shirt number for Chelsea during the 2016-2017 season?

10. Cesc Fabregas is what nationality?

11. Cesc Fabregas was signed by Chelsea from which club?

12. Charlie Cooke became Chelsea most expensive player in which year?

13. Charlie Cooke broke Chelsea transfer record at the time when he joined from which club?

14. Charlie Cooke joined Chelsea and became their most expensive player. What was the transfer fee?

15. Charlie Cooke wore which shirt number in the 1967 FA Cup

Final?

16. Chelsea first lifted the League Cup in which year?

17. Chelsea beat Manchester United by how many points in the 2005-2006 season?

18. Chelsea paid nearly £30 million to which Italian club in January 2015 for Juan Cuadrado?

19. Chelsea signed Ed De Goey from which club?

20. Chelsea signed Peter Cech from which French Club?

Answers

1. 1950s
2. 1963-64
3. Serbia
4. 1v0
5. 1
6. 2000
7. 1999-2000
8. Nigerian
9. 5
10. Spanish
11. Barcelona
12. 1966
13. Dundee
14. £72,000
15. 7
16. 1965
17. 1
18. Fiorentina
19. Feyenoord
20. Rennes

Round 3

1. Chelsea sold David Luiz in 2014 for £50 million to which club?

2. Chelsea were crowned league champions on how many occasions in the 1970s?

3. Chelsea won the 1955 League title by how many points?

4. Chelsea won the Community Shield for the first time in what year?

5. Chelsea won the Full Members Cup for the second time in 1990, beating which team in the final?

6. Chelsea won the Full Members cup in 1986. Who did they beat 5-4 in the final?

7. Chelsea won the League Cup for the third time in what year?

8. Chelsea won the Second Division title for the first time in what year?

9. Chelsea won the Second Division title in 1989 with how many points?

10. Chelsea won their first Europa League/UEFA Cup in which year?

11. Chelsea won their first League title in which year?

12. Chelsea won their fourth League Cup in what year?

13. Chelsea won their fourth League title in which year?

14. Chelsea paid £30.2 million for which Ukrainian players?

15. Chris Sutton became Chelsea most expensive player in which year?

16. Chris Sutton broke Chelsea transfer record at the time when he joined from which club?

17. Chris Sutton signed for Chelsea during which season?

18. Before joining Chelsea Chris Sutton won the Premier League with which club?

19. Chris Sutton left Chelsea in which year?

20. Chris Sutton's only league goal for Chelsea was against whom?

Answers

1. PSG

2. 0

3. 4

4. 1955

5. Middlesbrough

6. Manchester City

7. 2005

8. 1984

9. 99

10. 2013

11. 1954-1955

12. 2007

13. 2010

14. Andriy Shevchenko

15. 1999

16. Blackburn Rovers

17. 1999-2000

18. Blackburn Rovers

19. 2000

20. Manchester United

Round 1

1. By how many points did Chelsea win the 2004-2005 Premier League title?

2. Adrian Mutu was signed from which club?

3. Against which team did Gordon Durie score five goals in a famous 1989 league match?

4. Albert Ferrer, who played for Chelsea in the 2000s, was what nationality?

5. Allan Harris wore which shirt number in the 1967 FA Cup Final?

6. Andre Villas Boas was appointed Chelsea manager in which year?

7. Andreas Christensen was loaned to which team for the 2016-2017 season?

8. Andrew Wilson became Chelsea's most expensive player in which year?

9. Andrew Wilson was once Chelsea's record singing. How much did he cost?

10. Andy Myers left Chelsea in which season?

11. Ashley Cole joined Chelsea in which year?

12. Asmir Begovic wore which shirt number for Chelsea during the 2016-2017 season?

13. At which stadium did Chelsea beat Watford 5-1 in the 1970 FA Cup Semi Final?

14. Avram Grant was appointed as Chelsea manager in which year?

15. Baba Rahman was loaned to which team for the 2016-2017 season?

16. Bob McRoberts became Chelsea's most expensive player in which year?

17. Bob Microburst was once Chelsea's record singing. How much did he cost?

18. Bob Turnbull was the top scorer for Chelsea in which season?

19. Bobby Gould took charge of Chelsea in the 1980s for how many games?

20. Bobby Tambling wore which shirt number in the 1967 FA Cup Final?

Answers

1. 12

2. Parma

3. Walsall

4. Spanish

5. 2

6. 2011

7. Borussia Mönchengladbach

8. 1923

9. £6,500

10. 1999-2000

11. 2014

12. 1

13. White Hart Lane

14. 2007

15. Schalke 04

16. 1905

17. £100

18. 1926-27

19. 2

20. 10

Round 2

1. Bobby Tambling made his Chelsea debut in what decade?

2. Bobby Tambling was the top scorer for Chelsea in which season?

3. Branislav Ivanovic is from which country?

4. By what score did Chelsea beat Real Madrid in the 1998 UEFA Super Cup?

5. Carlo Ancelotti won the Premier League with Chelsea on how many occasions?

6. Carlo Cudicini signed for Chelsea in which year?

7. Carlo Cudicini signed for Chelsea during which season?

8. Celestine Babayaro, who played for Chelsea in the 2000s, was what nationality?

9. Cesc Fabregas wore which shirt number for Chelsea during the 2016-2017 season?

10. Cesc Fabregas is what nationality?

11. Cesc Fabregas was signed by Chelsea from which club?

12. Charlie Cooke became Chelsea most expensive player in which year?

13. Charlie Cooke broke Chelsea transfer record at the time when he joined from which club?

14. Charlie Cooke joined Chelsea and became their most expensive player. What was the transfer fee?

15. Charlie Cooke wore which shirt number in the 1967 FA Cup Final?

16. Chelsea first lifted the League Cup in which year?

17. Chelsea beat Manchester United by how many points in the 2005-2006 season?

18. Chelsea paid nearly £30 million to which Italian club in January 2015 for Juan Cuadrado?

19. Chelsea signed Ed De Goey from which club?

20. Chelsea signed Peter Cech from which French Club?

Answers

1. 1950s

2. 1963-64

3. Serbia

4. 1v0

5. 1

6. 2000

7. 1999-2000

8. Nigerian

9. 5

10. Spanish

11. Barcelona

12. 1966

13. Dundee

14. £72,000

15. 7

16. 1965

17. 1

18. Fiorentina

19. Feyenoord

20. Rennes

Round 3

1. Chelsea sold David Luiz in 2014 for £50 million to which club?

2. Chelsea were crowned league champions on how many occasions in the 1970s?

3. Chelsea won the 1955 League title by how many points?

4. Chelsea won the Community Shield for the first time in what year?

5. Chelsea won the Full Members Cup for the second time in 1990, beating which team in the final?

6. Chelsea won the Full Members cup in 1986. Who did they beat 5-4 in the final?

7. Chelsea won the League Cup for the third time in what year?

8. Chelsea won the Second Division title for the first time in what year?

9. Chelsea won the Second Division title in 1989 with how many points?

10. Chelsea won their first Europa League/UEFA Cup in which year?

11. Chelsea won their first League title in which year?

12. Chelsea won their fourth League Cup in what year?

13. Chelsea won their fourth League title in which year?

14. Chelsea paid £30.2 million for which Ukrainian players?

15. Chris Sutton became Chelsea most expensive player in which year?

16. Chris Sutton broke Chelsea transfer record at the time when he joined from which club?

17. Chris Sutton signed for Chelsea during which season?

18. Before joining Chelsea Chris Sutton won the Premier League with which club?

19. Chris Sutton left Chelsea in which year?

20. Chris Sutton's only league goal for Chelsea was against whom?

Answers

1. PSG

2. 0

3. 4

4. 1955

5. Middlesbrough

6. Manchester City

7. 2005

8. 1984

9. 99

10. 2013

11. 1954-1955

12. 2007

13. 2010

14. Andriy Shevchenko

15. 1999

16. Blackburn Rovers

17. 1999-2000

18. Blackburn Rovers

19. 2000

20. Manchester United

Round 4

1. Claude Makelele was signed from which club?

2. Clive Walker was the top scorer for Chelsea in which season?

3. Damien Duff became Chelsea most expensive player in which year?

4. Damien Duff broke Chelsea transfer record at the time when he joined from which club?

5. Daniel Sturridge netted how many times for Chelsea in the 2011-2012 season?

6. Dave Beasant became Chelsea most expensive player in which year?

7. Dave Beasant was the most expensive player to join Chelsea upon signing. How much was he?

8. Dave Sexton was in charge at Chelsea for how many years?

9. Dave Sexton won the FA Cup with Chelsea in what season?

10. David Calderhead managed Chelsea for how many matches between 1907 and 1933?

11. David Hay became Chelsea most expensive player in which year?

12. David Hay broke Chelsea transfer record at the time when he joined from which club?

13. David Hay joined Chelsea and became their most expensive player. What was the transfer fee?

14. David Speedie scored how many goals in the Full Members Cup Final in 1986?

15. David Webb was a manger of Chelsea in which decade?

16. Diego Costa wore which shirt number for Chelsea during the 2016-2017 season?

17. Dennis Wise became Chelsea most expensive player in which year?

18. Dennis Wise was the most expensive player to join Chelsea upon signing. How much was he?

19. Dennis Wise played for Chelsea in how many different seasons?

20. Dennis wise played his final game for Chelsea in what year?

Answers

1. Real Madrid

2. 1979-80

3. 2003

4. Blackburn Rovers

5. 11

6. 1989

7. £725,000

8. 7

9. 1970

10. 966

11. 1974

12. Celtic

13. £225,000

14. 3

15. 1990s

16. 19

17. 1990

18. £1.6 million

19. 11

20. 2001

Round 5

1. Derek Kevan became Chelsea's most expensive player in which year?

2. Derek Kevan broke Chelsea's transfer record at the time when he joined from which club?

3. Derek Kevan joined Chelsea and became their most expensive player. What was the transfer fee?

4. Didier Deschamps left Chelsea in which year?

5. Didier Deschamps signed for Chelsea during which season?

6. Didier Deschamps was signed by Chelsea from which club?

7. Didier Drogba became Chelsea most expensive player in which year?

8. Didier Drogba was the top scorer for Chelsea in which of season?

9. Didier Drogba broke Chelsea's transfer record at the time when he joined from which club?

10. Didier Drogba appeared in many League Cup finals for Chelsea. But how many goals did he score in these appearances?

11. Didier Drogba was bought by Chelsea in 2004 for how much?

12. Didier Drogba was originally signed by Chelsea from which French club?

13. Diego Costa is what nationality?

14. Diego Costa was the top scorer for Chelsea in which season?

15. Diego Costa was signed in 2014 from which Spanish club?

16. Dmitri Kharine, who played for Chelsea in the 1990s, was what nationality?

17. During 1971 and 1974 John Hollins made a record number of Chelsea appearances. How many?

18. During his first run with the club, how many trophies did Jose Mourinho lift with Chelsea?

19. Ed De Goey, who played for Chelsea in the 2000s, was what nationality?

20. Eddie Newton left Chelsea in which season?

Answers

1. 1962

2. WBA

3. £45,000

4. 2000

5. 1999-2000

6. Juventus

7. 2004

8. 2006-07

9. Marseille

10. 4

11. £24 million

12. Marseille

13. Spanish

14. 2014-15

15. Atletico Madrid

16. Russian

17. 167

18. 6

19. Dutch

20. 1999-2000

Round 6

1. Form what club did Chelsea sign Frank Lamped?

2. Former manager Billy Burrell was what nationality?

3. Frank Lamped played for Chelsea in a record number of European games. How many?

4. Frank Leboeuf became Chelsea most expensive player in which year?

5. Frank Leboeuf was the most expensive player to join Chelsea upon signing. How much did he cost?

6. Frank Lebouef, who played for Chelsea in the 2000s, was what nationality?

7. Frank Pearson was the top scorer for Chelsea in which season?

8. Frank Sinclair, who played for Chelsea in the 1990s, was what nationality?

9. Fred Rouse became Chelsea most expensive player in which year?

10. Fred Rouse was once Chelsea record singing. How much did he cost?

11. From which club did Asmir Begovic join Chelsea?

12. From which club did Chelsea sign Hernan Crespo?

13. From which club did Chelsea sign Gianfranco Zola?

14. From which club did Chelsea sign Jose Bosingwa?

15. From which club did Chelsea sign Kerry Dixon?

16. From which club did Chelsea sign Nicolas Anelka?

17. From which club did Chelsea sign prolific scorer Roy Bentley?

18. From which club did Chelsea sin Marcos Alonso?

19. From which club did Frank Leboeuf join Chelsea?

20. From which club did Joe Cole join Chelsea?

Answers

1. West Ham United
2. Scottish
3. 117
4. 1996
5. £2.5 million
6. French
7. 1905-06
8. Jamaican
9. 1907
10. £900
11. Stoke City
12. Inter Milan
13. Parma
14. Porto
15. Reading
16. Bolton
17. Newcastle United
18. Fiorentina
19. Strasbourg
20. West Ham United

.

Round 7

1. From which club did Chelsea sign Dennis Wise?

2. From which Scottish club did Chelsea sign Steve Clarke?

3. Gabriele Ambrosetti signed for Chelsea during which season?

4. Gary Cahill wore which shirt number for Chelsea during the 2016-2017 season?

5. Geoff Hurst managed Chelsea for how many games?

6. George Hilsdon was a prolific scorer for Chelsea and made his debut in what year?

7. George Mills was the top scorer for Chelsea in which season?

8. George Weah signed for Chelsea during which season?

9. George Weah was signed by Chelsea from which club?

10. Gianfranco Zola was the top scorer for Chelsea in which of these season?

11. Gianluca Vialli left Chelsea as manager in what year?

12. Gianluca Vialli won how many trophies as Chelsea manager?

13. Glen Johnson joined Chelsea in which year?

14. Glenn Hoddle was Chelsea manager during which decade?

15. Gordon Durie became Chelsea most expensive player in which year?

16. Gordon Durie broke Chelsea transfer record at the time when he joined from which club?

17. Gordon Durie was the top scorer for Chelsea in which of these season?

18. Gordon Durie was the most expensive player to join Chelsea upon signing. How much did he cost?

19. Graeme Le Saux became Chelsea most expensive player in which year?

20. Graeme Le Saux broke Chelsea transfer record at the time when he joined from which club?

Answers

1. Wimbledon
2. St Mirren
3. 1999-2000
4. 24
5. 81
6. 1906
7. 1937-38
8. 1999-2000
9. AC Milan
10. 1998-99
11. 2000
12. 5
13. 2003
14. 1990s
15. 1986
16. Hibernian
17. 1990-91
18. £380,000
19. 1997
20. Blackburn Rovers

Round 8

1. Graham Moore became Chelsea most expensive player in which year?

2. Graham Moore broke Chelsea transfer record at the time when he joined from which club?

3. Graham Moore joined Chelsea and became their most expensive player. What was the transfer fee?

4. Graham Rix took over Chelsea for two games after which managers departure?

5. Gustavo Poyet, who played for Chelsea in the 2000s, was what nationality?

6. Gus Hiddink guided Chelsea to how many trophies?

7. Gus Hiddink was both hired and fired as manager of Chelsea in what year?

8. Happy is the middle name of which Chelsea player?

9. How many penalties did Chelsea concede in the 1994 FA Cup final?

10. How many goals did John Hollins score in his Chelsea career?

11. How many English players started for Chelsea in the 1994 FA Cup Final?

12. How many appearances did Branislav Ivanovic make in his Chelsea career?

13. How many appearances did Roberto Di Matteo make for Chelsea?

14. How many appearances did Petr Cech make for Chelsea?

15. How many appearances did Frank Lamped make for Chelsea?

16. How many appearances in total did Dennis Wise make for Chelsea?

17. How many appearances did John Hollins make for Chelsea in his career?

18. How many appearances did John Terry make for Chelsea?

19. How many Champions League titles did John Terry win with Chelsea?

20. How many clean sheets did Ed De Goey keep in the 1999-2000 season?

Answers

1. 1961
2. Cardiff City
3. £35,000
4. Gianluca Vialli
5. Uruguayan
6. 1
7. 2009
8. Kurt Zouma
9. 2
10. 69
11. 4
12. 377
13. 175
14. 486
15. 429
16. 445
17. 592
18. 713
19. 1
20. 27

Round 9

1. How many clean sheets did Petr Cech keep in all competitions during his time at Chelsea?

2. How many consecutive appearances did Frank Lampard play for Chelsea in his record-breaking run?

3. How many England caps did Frank Lampard win whilst playing for Chelsea?

4. How many FA Cup finals did Chelsea lose up until 2016?

5. How many FA Cup games did record breaker Ron Harris play in for Chelsea?

6. How many FA Cups did John Terry win with Chelsea?

7. How many games did Andre Villas-Boas serve as Chelsea manager?

8. How many games did Avram Grant have as Chelsea manager?

9. How many games did Carlo Ancelotti have as manager of Chelsea?

10. How many games did Dmitri Kharine play for Chelsea?

11. How many games did Gus Hiddink have in charge of Chelsea?

12. How many games was Ruud Gullit in charge of Chelsea?

13. How many goals did Andriy Shevchenko score during his time at Chelsea?

14. How many goals did Andriy Shevchenko score in his first 50 games for Chelsea?

15. How many goals did Branilsav Ivanovic score in his Chelsea career?

16. How many goals did Chelsea concede in the final of the 1998 UEFA Cup Winners Cup?

17. How many goals did Didier Drogba score in the 2009-2010 season, a club Premier League record?

18. How many goals did Frank Lampard score for Chelsea in his career?

19. How many goals did Frank Lamped score in his Chelsea career?

20. How many goals did George Hilsdon score in a FA Cup Match against Worksop town, a club record?

Answers

1. 220

2. 164

3. 103

4. 4

5. 64

6. 3

7. 40

8. 54

9. 109

10. 146

11. 22

12. 83

13. 22

14. 14

15. 34

16. 0

17. 29

18. 311

19. 147

20. 6

Round 10

1. How many goals did Jimmy Greaves score in his record breaking 1961 season?

2. How many goals did Jimmy Floyd Hasselbaink net in a 2000 win over Coventry City?

3. How many goals did John Terry score during has Chelsea career?

4. How many goals did Kerry Dixon score in his Chelsea career?

5. How many goals did Peter Osgood score during his Chelsea career?

6. How many goals did Roberto Di Matteo score in his first season with Chelsea?

7. How many goals did top scorer Eden Hazard score in the 2013-2014 season?

8. How many goals did Chelsea score in the final of the 1998 UEFA Cup Winners Cup?

9. How many goals were Chelsea ahead of Sheffield Wednesday, a figure which meant they won the 1984 Second Division Title?

10. How many goals in total did Roberto Di Matteo score for Chelsea?

11. How many League titles did Branislav Invanovic win with Chelsea?

12. How many League titles did Chelsea in in the 1950s?

13. How many league titles did Chelsea win in the 1950s?

14. How many league titles did John Terry win with Premier League?

15. How many league titles did Jose Mourinho win during his first spell at Chelsea?

16. How many months did Luiz Felipe Scolari last as manager of Chelsea?

17. How many penalties did Chelsea miss in the shootout in the 2008 UEFA Champions League Final?

18. How many points did Chelsea finish ahead of Manchester United in the 2005-2006 season?

19. How many points did Chelsea gain in their league winning season in 2004-2005?

20. How many Scottish players started for Chelsea in the 1967 FA Cup final?

Answers

1. 43

2. 4

3. 66

4. 193

5. 150

6. 9

7. 14

8. 1

9. 22

10. 26

11. 2

12. 1

13. 1

14. 4

15. 2

16. 7

17. 2

18. 8

19. 95

20. 3

Round 11

1. How many seasons did Andriy Shevchenko spend with Chelsea?

2. How many seasons did Jimmy Floyd Hasselbaink spend with Chelsea?

3. How many seasons did Graeme Le Saux spend with Chelsea?

4. How many seconds did it take for Roberto Di Matteo to score in the 1997 FA Cup final?

5. How many seconds did it take Keith Weller to score in the 1970 League Cup Final against Middlesbrough?

6. How many times were Chelsea crowned league Champions in the 1980s?

7. How many times between 2000 and 2010 did Chelsea win the Community Shield?

8. How many times between 2000-2010 were Chelsea crowned League Champions?

9. How many times did Ashley Cole win the FA Cup with Chelsea?

10. How many times did Andriy Shevchenko play for Chelsea?

11. How many times did Branislav Ivanonvic win the FA Cup with Chelsea?

12. How many times did Chelsea win the Cup Winners Cup?

13. How many times did Chelsea win the FA Cup in the 1970s?

14. How many times did Chelsea win the FA Cup in the 20th Century?

15. How many times did Chelsea win the league title in the 1990s?

16. How many times did Chelsea win the League title in the 2000s?

17. How many times did Chelsea win the Second Division Title in the 1980s?

18. How many times did Chelsea win the Cup Winners Cup?

19. How many times did Chelsea win the FA Cup in the 1970s?

20. How many times did Dennis Wise win the FA cup with Chelsea?

Answers

1. 3

2. 4

3. 6

4. 42

5. 12

6. 0

7. 3

8. 3

9. 4

10. 77

11. 3

12. 2

13. 1

14. 2

15. 0

16. 3

17. 2

18. 2

19. 1

20. 2

Round 12

1. How many times did Didier Drogba score in the FA Cup Final during his multiple appearances for Chelsea?

2. How many times did Peter Osgood play for Chelsea?

3. How many times did Steve Clarke play for Chelsea?

4. How many times in the 1980s did Chelsea win the Second division?

5. How many times in the 20th Century did Chelsea win the Community Shield?

6. How many trophies did Marcel Desailly win with Chelsea?

7. How many trophies did Roberto Di Matteo win with Chelsea?

8. How many years did Ashley Cole spend at Chelsea?

9. How many years did Frank Lamped spent with Chelsea?

10. How many years did Peter Cech spend with Chelsea?

11. How many years did Tommy Docherty manage Chelsea?

12. How many years elapsed between Chelsea's first and second FA Cup wins?

13. How many years elapsed between Chelsea's first and second League Title wins?

14. How many years passed between Chelsea's first and second Cup Winners Cup victories?

15. How many years passed between Chelsea's first and second League Cup Final wins?

16. How much did Ken Bates pay for Chelsea in 1982?

17. How much did Chelsea pay for Nicolas Anelka?

18. How much did Chelsea pay Stoke City for Asmir Begovic?

19. How much did Chelsea pay Fiorentina for Marco Alonso?

20. How much did Chelsea pay Rennes for Petr Cech?

Answers

1. 4
2. 298
3. 421
4. 2
5. 0
6. 1
7. 2
8. 8
9. 13
10. 11
11. 6
12. 27
13. 49
14. 27
15. 33
16. £1
17. £15 million
18. £8 million
19. £24 million
20. £7 million

Round 13

1. How much did Ken Bates sell Chelsea for in 2003?

2. How old was Ian Hamilton when he became Chelsea's youngest player in a 1967 match?

3. How old was Mark Schwarzer when he became Chelsea's oldest ever player in a 2014 Premier League game?

4. Hughie Gallacher became Chelsea most expensive player in which year?

5. Hughie Gallacher broke Chelsea's transfer record at the time when he joined from which club?

6. Hughie Gallacher was once Chelsea record singing. How much did he cost?

7. Hughie Gallacher was the top scorer for Chelsea in which season?

8. Ian Hutchinson wore which shirt number in the 1970 FA Cup Final?

9. In 1999, who was voted Chelsea's player of the Year?

10. In 2001 who was voted Chelsea's player of the Year?

11. In 2003 who became Chelsea's record signing when they paid Blackburn Rovers £17 million?

12. In 2008, which Chelsea player signed a deal to make him the highest paid player in the league?

13. In 2014, who became the first Premier League player to net an assist in six consecutive games?

14. In the 1960s, Chelsea won the League title on how many occasions?

15. In total how many games did Andriy Shevchenko score in his Chelsea career?

16. In total, how many FA Cup finals did Chelsea play in between their founding and 2016?

17. In what city did Chelsea win the 1998 UEFA Super Cup?

18. In what city did Chelsea win the 2012 Champions League?

19. In what decade did Jimmy Greaves net a record 43 goals for Chelsea?

20. In what decade did Steve Clarke make his Chelsea debut?

Answers

1. £140 million

2. 16

3. 41

4. 1930

5. Newcastle United

6. £10,000

7. 1930-31

8. 10

9. Gianfranco Zola

10. John Terry

11. Damien Duff

12. Frank Lampard

13. Cesc Fabregas

14. 0

15. 22

16. 11

17. Monaco

18. Munich

19. 1960s

20. 1980s

Round 14

1. In what decade was Ian Porterfield manager of Chelsea?

2. In what decade was Tommy Docherty manager of Chelsea?

3. In what season was Nicolas Anelka the top scorer for Chelsea in the league?

4. In what year did Chelsea re-sign Didier Drogba?

5. In what year did Asmir Begovic join Chelsea?

6. In what year did Branislav Invanovic join Chelsea?

7. In what year did Carlo Ancelotti leave Chelsea?

8. In what year did Cesc Fabregas join Chelsea?

9. In what year did Chelsea pay £24 million for Michael Essien?

10. In what year did Chelsea purchase Juan Mata?

11. In what year did Chelsea win the Europa League for the first time?

12. In what year did Chelsea win the FA Cup for the first time?

13. In what year did Chelsea win the UEFA Super Cup for the first time?

14. In what year did Chelsea win their only Super Cup?

15. In what year did Chelsea lose the so-called Cockney Cup Final?

16. In what year did Chris Sutton become Chelsea's record signing?

17. In what year did Didier Drogba first join Chelsea?

18. In what year did Dmitri Kharine join Chelsea?

19. In what year did Ed De Goey play his final game for Chelsea?

20. In what year did Frank Lampard join Chelsea?

Answers

1. 1990s

2. 1960s

3. 2008-2009

4. 2014

5. 2015

6. 2008

7. 2011

8. 2014

9. 2005

10. 2011

11. 2013

12. 1970

13. 1998

14. 1998

15. 1967

16. 1999

17. 2004

18. 1992

19. 2003

20. 2001

Round 15

1. In what year did Frank Lampard play his final game for Chelsea?

2. In what year did Gus Hiddink manage Chelsea to FA Cup success?

3. In what year did Joe Cole make his Chelsea debut?

4. In what year did John Hollins make his Chelsea debut?

5. In what year did John Terry make his full Chelsea debut?

6. In what year did Jose Mourinho return to Chelsea for his second spell as manager?

7. In what year did Kerry Dixon make his final appearance for Chelsea?

8. In what year did Man United beat Chelsea 4-0 in the FA Cup Final?

9. In what year did Man Utd defeat Chelsea in the Champions League Final?

10. In what year did Marcel Desailly join Chelsea?

11. In what year did Nicolas Anelka join Chelsea?

12. In what year did Nicolas Anelka play his firstgame for Chelsea?

13. In what year did Nicolas Anelka play his final game for Chelsea?

14. In what year did Petr Cech clash with Stephen Hunt leading to his infamous head injury?

15. In what year did Ron Harris play his first game fir Chelsea?

16. In what year did Salomon Kalou join Chelsea?

17. In what year did Ted Drake manager Chelsea to become Premier League Champions?

18. In what year did Terry Venables make his debut for Chelsea?

19. In what year did Tommy Docherty leave Chelsea as manager?

20. In what year did Zola join Chelsea?

Answers

1. 2014

2. 2009

3. 2003

4. 1963

5. 1998

6. 2013

7. 1992

8. 1994

9. 2008

10. 1998

11. 2008

12. 2008

13. 2011

14. 2006

15. 1961

16. 2006

17. 1955

18. 1960

19. 1967

20. 1996

Round 16

1. In what year did Chelsea beat Leeds United 2-1 in a cup final replay?

2. In what year did Andriy Shevchenko sign for Chelsea?

3. In what year was Carlo Ancelotti appointed manager of Chelsea?

4. In what year was Claudio Ranieri appointed as Chelsea boss?

5. In what year was Dave Sexton appointed as Chelsea manager?

6. In what year was Geoff Hurst announced as manager of Chelsea?

7. In what year was Glenn Hoddle appointed as Chelsea manager?

8. In what year was John Terry born?

9. In what year did Chelsea beat Liverpool 2-1 in the FA Cup Final?

10. In which city did Chelsea win the 1998 Cup Winners Cup?

11. In which city did Chelsea win the 2013 Europa League?

12. In which city did Chelsea win the 1971 UEFA Cup Winners Cup?

13. In which city did the 2013 Europa League final take place?

14. In which city did Chelsea win the 1998 UEFA Cup Winners Cup?

15. In which city did Chelsea lose the 2008 UEFA Champions League Final?

16. In which two years did Chelsea win their only back to back titles?

17. In which year did Branislav Ivanonvic leave Chelsea?

18. Isaiah Brown was loaned to which team for the 2016-2017 season?

19. Jack Cook became Chelsea most expensive player in which year?

20. Jack Cook was once Chelsea record singing. How much did he cost?

Answers

1. 1970

2. 2006

3. 2009

4. 2000

5. 1967

6. 1979

7. 1993

8. 1980

9. 2012

10. Stockholm

11. Amsterdam

12. Piraeus

13. Amsterdam

14. Stockholm

15. Moscow

16. 2005 and 206

17. 2017

18. Huddersfield Town

19. 1919

20. £2,500

Round 17

1. Jack Cook was the top scorer for Chelsea in which season?

2. Jake Slater was loaned to which team for the 2016-2017 season?

3. Jakob Kjeldbjerg, who played for Chelsea in the 1990s, was what nationality?

4. Jamal Blackman was loaned to which team for the 2016-2017 season?

5. Jerrel is the real first name of which Chelsea legend?

6. Jesper Gronkjaer signed for Chelsea in which year?

7. Jimmy Floyd Hasslebaink was the top scorer for Chelsea in which season?

8. Jimmy Floyd Hasslebaink left Chelsea in 2004 and joined which team?

9. Jimmy Greaves was the top scorer for Chelsea in which season?

10. Jimmy Floyd Hasslebaink became Chelsea's most expensive player in which year?

11. John Dempsey wore which shirt number in the 1970 FA Cup Final?

12. John Hollins wore which shirt number in the 1967 FA Cup Final?

13. John Hollins played for Chelsea for how many years?

14. John Hollins potted which player in a local tournament on the Isle of Jersey?

15. John Neal signed which players for Chelsea in 1983?

16. John Spencer was the top scorer for Chelsea in which season?

17. Jose Bosingwa left Chelsea in 2012 to join which club?

18. Jose Mourinho initially replaced whom as Chelsea manager?

19. Juan Mata netted how many goals in his Chelsea career?

20. Juan Mata played how many games for Chelsea during the 2012-2013 season, a record for the club?

Answers

1. 1920-21

2. Bristol Rovers

3. Danish

4. Wycombe Wanderers

5. Jimmy Floyd Hasselbaink

6. 2000

7. 2003-04

8. Middlesbrough

9. 1958-59

10. 2000

11. 5

12. 4

13. 12

14. Graeme Le Saux

15. Kerry Dixon

16. 1995-96

17. QPR

18. Claudio Ranieri

19. 33

20. 64

Round 18

1. Juan Mata was bought for £23 million from which club?

2. Ken Bates was born in which year?

3. Kerry Dixon was the top scorer for Chelsea in which season?

4. Kerry Dixon played how many times for Chelsea?

5. Kurt Zouma wore which shirt number for Chelsea during the 2016-2017 season?

6. Who did Chelsea beat to win the 2005 League Cup final?

7. Who did Chelsea beat to win the 2007 League Cup final?

8. Who scored Chelsea's first goal in the 2015 League Cup final?

9. Luiz Felipe Scolari was appointed Chelsea manager in what year?

10. Luiz Felipe Scolari was fired as Chelsea manager in what year?

11. Billy Birrell was replaced as manager by who, in 1952?

12. Danny Blanchflower was replaced as manager by who, in 1979?

13. Bobby Campbell was replaced as manager by who, in 1991?

14. Marcos Alonso is what nationality?

15. Marcos Alonso wore which shirt number for Chelsea during the 2016-2017 season?

16. Mario Melchiot signed for Chelsea during which season?

17. Mario Melchiot was signed by Chelsea from which club?

18. Mario Paslic was loaned to which team for the 2016-2017 season?

19. Mario Stanic signed for Chelsea in which year?

20. Mario Stanic was signed by Chelsea from which club?

Answers

1. Valencia

2. 1931

3. 1983-84

4. 420

5. 5

6. Liverpool

7. Arsenal

8. John Terry

9. 2008

10. 2009

11. Ted Drake

12. Geoff Hurst

13. Ian Porterfield

14. Spanish

15. 3

16. 1999-2000

17. Ajax

18. AC Milan

19. 2000

20. Parma

Round 19

1. Mario Stanic, who played for Chelsea in the 2000s, was what nationality?

2. Mark Bosnich was signed by Chelsea from which club?

3. Michael Duberry left Chelsea in which season?

4. Michael Essien broke Chelsea transfer record at the time when he joined from which club?

5. What year did Michael Essien join Chelsea?

6. Michael Essien was bought by Chelsea for how much?

7. Mickey Hazard became Chelsea most expensive player in which year?

8. Mickey Hazard broke Chelsea transfer record at the time when he joined from which club?

9. Mickey Hazard joined Chelsea and became their most expensive player. What was the transfer fee?

10. Mikael Forssell, who played for Chelsea in the 2000s, was what nationality?

11. N'Golo Kante wore which shirt number for Chelsea during the 2016-2017 season?

12. Nathan Ake wore which shirt number for Chelsea during the 2016-2017 season?

13. Nils Middelboe was the first player from outside the UK to play for Chelsea. What nationality was he?

14. Of his 22 games in charge, how many were wins for manager Gus Hiddink?

15. On how many occasions did Carlo Ancelotti win the FA Cup with Chelsea?

16. On how many occasions was Frank Lamped the top scorer of the league season for Chelsea?

17. Paul Furlong was the most expensive player to join Chelsea upon signing. How much did he cost?

18. Paul Furlong became Chelsea most expensive player in which year?

19. Paul Furlong broke Chelsea transfer record at the time when he joined from which club?

20. Pedro wore which shirt number for Chelsea during the 2016-2017 season?

Answers

1. Croatian

2. Manchester United

3. 1999-2000

4. Lyon

5. 2005

6. £24.4 million

7. 1985

8. Spurs

9. £300,000

10. Finnish

11. 7

12. 6

13. Danish

14. 16

15. 1

16. 5

17. £2.3 million

18. 1993

19. Watford

20. 11

Round 20

1. Robert Di Matteo joined Chelsea from which club?

2. Robert Flack became Chelsea most expensive player in which year?

3. Robert Flack broke Chelsea transfer record at the time when he joined from which club?

4. Robert Flack was the most expensive player to join Chelsea upon signing. How much did he cost?

5. Roberto Di Matteo, who played for Chelsea in the 2000s, was what his nationality?

6. Roberto Di Matteo had what win % as Chelsea manager?

7. Roberto Di Matteo was both appointed and sacked during which year?

8. Ron Harris played how many times for Chelsea during his career?

9. Roy Bentley made his Chelsea debut in what year?

10. Roy Bentley scored how many times during his Chelsea career?

11. Roy Bentley was Chelsea's top scorer in how many different seasons?

12. Roy Bentley was the top scorer for Chelsea in which season?

13. Ruud Gullit was appointed as Chelsea manager in what year?

14. Salomon Kalou played his final game for Chelsea in which year?

15. Slabisa Jokanovic signed for Chelsea in which year?

16. Slavsia Jokanovic , who played for Chelsea in the 2000s, was what nationality?

17. Mario Paslic was loaned to which team for the 2016-2017 season?

18. Mario Stanic signed for Chelsea in which year?

19. Mario Stanic was signed by Chelsea from which club?

20. Steve Clarke, who played for Chelsea in the 1990s, was what nationality?

Answers

1. Lazio

2. 1992

3. Norwich City

4. £2.1 million

5. Italian

6. 57

7. 2012

8. 795

9. 1948

10. 150

11. 8

12. 1948-1949

13. 1996

14. 2012

15. 2000

16. Serbian

17. AC Milan

18. 2000

19. Parma

20. Scottish

Round 21

1. Steve Clarke joined Chelsea from which Scottish team?

2. Steve Kember became Chelsea most expensive player in which year?

3. Steve Kember broke Chelsea transfer record at the time when he joined from which club?

4. Steve Kember joined Chelsea and became their most expensive player. What was the transfer fee?

5. Tebily is the real surname of which Chelsea legend?

6. Tomas Kalas was loaned to which team for the 2016-2017 season?

7. Tommy Baldwin wore which shirt number in the 1970 FA Cup Final?

8. Tommy Docherty was appointed Chelsea manager in what year?

9. Tommy Langley was the top scorer for Chelsea in which of these season?

10. Tommy Lawton became Chelsea most expensive player in which year?

11. Tommy Lawton broke Chelsea transfer record at the time when he joined from which club?

12. Tommy Lawton was once Chelsea record singing. How much did he cost?

13. Tommy Meehan became Chelsea most expensive player in which year?

14. Tommy Meehan was once Chelsea record singing. How much did he cost?

15. Tony Dorigo became Chelsea most expensive player in which year?

16. Tony Cascarino, who played for Chelsea in the 1990s, was what nationality?

17. Tony Dorigo broke Chelsea transfer record at the time when he joined from which club?

18. Tony Dorigo was the most expensive player to join Chelsea upon signing. How much was he?

19. Tony Hateley broke Chelsea transfer record at the time when he joined from which club?

20. Tony Hateley joined Chelsea and became their most expensive player. What was the transfer fee?

Answers

1. St Mirren

2. 1971

3. Crystal Palace

4. £170,000

5. Didier Drogba

6. Fulham

7. 7

8. 1961

9. 1977-78

10. 1945

11. Everton

12. £14,000

13. 1920

14. £3,300

15. 1987

16. Irish

17. Aston Villa

18. £475,000

19. Aston Villa

20. £100,000

Round 22

1. Tony Hateley wore which shirt number in the 1967 FA Cup Final?

2. Who scored a penalty in a League cup final against Chelsea?

3. Who scored a record 211 goals in his Chelsea career?

4. Tore Andre Flo netted how many goals for Chelsea as their top scorer in 1999-2000?

5. Who scored 13 goals in 44 matches in his first Season with Chelsea in 1990-1991?

6. Who scored 23 goals in 35 games in the 2000-2001 season?

7. Who scored 3 goals as Chelsea game from Behind to bear Wolves 5-2 at Stamford Bridge in 2004?

8. Who scored 3 goals in a 2002 4-0 drubbing of Spurs?

9. Who scored 4 goals in a 1997 league game against Barnsley?

10. What nationality was Tommy Docherty?

11. Victor Moses wore which shirt number for Chelsea during the 2016-2017 season?

12. What colour shirts did Chelsea wear in the 2009 FA Cup Final?

13. What is Kurt Zouma's middle name?

14. What nationality if former Chelsea player Jose Bosingwa?

15. What nationality is former Chelsea manager Avram Grant?

16. What nationality is former Chelsea manager Ruud Gullit?

17. What nationality is Kurt Zouma?

18. What nationality is Nicolas Anelka?

19. What nationality is two-time Chelsea manager Jose Mourinho?

20. What nationality was Adrian Mutu?

Answers

1. 9
2. Terry Venables
3. Frank Lampard
4. 10
5. Dennis Wise
6. Jimmy Floyd Hasselbaink
7. Jimmy Floyd Hasselbaink
8. Jimmy Floyd Hasselbaink
9. Gianluca Vialli
10. Scottish
11. 15
12. Yellow
13. Happy
14. Portuguese
15. Israeli
16. Dutch
17. French
18. French
19. Portuguese
20. Romania

Round 23

1. What nationality was Chelsea's first manager John Tait Robertson?

2. What nationality was Eddie McCredie who played over 400 games for Chelsea?

3. What nationality was former Chelsea manager David Calderhead?

4. What nationality was former coach Gus Hiddink?

5. What nationality was former manager Andre Villas Boas?

6. What nationality was former manager Carlo Ancelotti?

7. What nationality was former manager Rafael Benitez?

8. What nationality was Tommy Docherty?

9. What nationality is Chelsea Legend Marcel Desailly?

10. What was Andre Villas Boas win % in competitive games at Chelsea?

11. What was the score at full time in the 2008 UEFA Champions League Final?

12. What was the score in the 1970 FA Cup Final replay?

13. What was the score in the 1994 FA Cup Final when Chelsea played Man Utd?

14. What was the score in the 1997 FA Cup Final between Chelsea and Middlesbrough?

15. What was the score in the 2005 League Cup Final when Chelsea defeated Liverpool?

16. What was the score in the 2009 FA Cup Final between Chelsea and Everton?

17. What was the score in the famous Full Members cup final game of 1986 between Chelsea and Manchester City?

18. What was the score in the original 1970 FA Cup Final between Chelsea and Leeds?

19. What was the score in the original final of the 1971 UEFA Cup Winners Cup?

20. What was the score when Chelsea beat Manchester United in the 2007 FA Cup Final?

Answers

1. Scottish

2. Scottish

3. Scottish

4. Dutch

5. Portuguese

6. Italian

7. Spanish

8. Scottish

9. French

10. 48

11. 1-1

12. 2-1

13. 4-0

14. 2-0

15. 3-2

16. 2-1

17. 5-4

18. 2-2

19. 1-1

20. 1-0

Round 24

1. What was the score when Chelsea defeated Benfica in the 2013 Europa League final?

2. What was the transfer free for Oscar when Chelsea bought him from International in 2012?

3. What as the score in the infamous "Cockney cup Final"?

4. When did Ashley Cole join Arsenal?

5. When did Celestine Babayaro join Chelsea?

6. When did Chelsea first play in the FA Cup final?

7. When did Chelsea first win the Cup Winners Cup?

8. When did Chelsea originally sign Didier Drogba?

9. When did Chelsea play in the last ever FA Cup Final to be played at the Old Wembley?

10. When did Chelsea win the Champions League for the first time?

11. When did Chelsea win the FA Cup for the first time?

12. When did Chelsea win the League Cup for the first time?

13. When did Chelsea win their first FA Cup?

14. When did Chelsea win their second League Title?

15. When did David Webb play his first game from Chelsea?

16. When did Dennis Wise join Chelsea?

17. When did Dmitri Kharine leave Chelsea?

18. When did Ed De Goey join Chelsea?

19. When did Frank Lamped make his Chelsea debut?

. 20 When did Frank Leboeuf join Chelsea?

Answers

1. 2-1

2. £25 Million

3. 2-1

4. 2006

5. 1997

6. 1915

7. 1971

8. 2004

9. 2000

10. 2012

11. 1970

12. 1965

13. 1970

14. 2005

15. 1968

16. 1990

17. 1999

18. 1997

19. 2001

20. 1996

Round 25

1. When did Frank Leboeuf play his final game for Chelsea?

2. When did Glen Johnson left Chelsea?

3. When did Hernan Crespo join Chelsea?

4. When did Hernan Crespo play his final game for Chelsea?

5. When did John Hollins make his Chelsea debut?

6. when did John Terry make his Chelsea debut?

7. When did Jose Bosingwa join Chelsea?

8. When did Jose Bosingwa leave Chelsea?

9. When did Ken Bates buy Chelsea?

10. When did Ken Bates sell Chelsea?

11. When did Kerry Dixon make his Chelsea debut?

12. When did Kerry Dixon play his final Chelsea game?

13. When did Peter Osgood play his final game for Chelsea?

14. When did Peter Osgood play his first game for Chelsea?

15. When did record breaking Chelsea player Ron Harris make his final appearance for the club?

16. When did Roberto Di Matteo play his final game for Chelsea?

17. When did Ron Harris play his final game for Chelsea?

18. When did Ron Harris, record appearance maker for Chelsea play his first game for the club?

19. When did Terry Venables play his final game for Chelsea?

20. When did Zola play his final game for Chelsea?

Answers

1. 2001

2. 2007

3. 2003

4. 2008

5. 1963

6. 1998

7. 2008

8. 2012

9. 1982

10. 2003

11. 1983

12. 1992

13. 1979

14. 1964

15. 1980

16. 2003

17. 1980

18. 1961

19. 1966

20. 2003

Round 26

1. When was Andre Villas- Boas sacked as Chelsea manager?

2. When were Chelsea crowned Champions for a third time?

3. When were Chelsea first crowned League Champions?

4. Where did Chelsea 1970 FA Cup final victory over Leeds United take place?

5. Where did Dmitri Kharine go when he left Chelsea in 1999?

6. Where did Ed De Goey go when he left Chelsea in 2003?

7. Where did John Terry go to on Loan in 2000?

8. Where did Petr Cech go when he left Chelsea in 2015?

9. Who joined Chelsea from Wimbledon in 1990?

10. Which Chelsea legend began his playing career at West Ham United?

11. Which Chelsea legend is also a children's author?

12. Which Chelsea legend was born in Romford in 1978?

13. Which Chelsea player holds the record has having won the most FA Cup medals in history?

14. Which Chelsea player is second to Ryan Giggs in all time Premier League assists?

15. Which Chelsea player was formerly on loan at Sunderland?

16. Which Chelsea legend was acquired from Rennes in 2004?

17. Which Chelsea player was injured in 2010 ruling him out of that year's World Cop?

18. Which Chelsea Legend was born in Barking in 1980?

19. Which club did Ron Harris join after Chelsea?

20. Which club signed Glen Johnson when he left Chelsea?

Answers

1. 2012

2. 2006

3. 1955

4. Old Trafford

5. Celtic

6. Stoke

7. Notts Forest

8. Arsenal

9. Dennis Wise

10. Frank Lampard

11. Frank Lampard

12. Frank Lampard

13. Ashley Cole

14. Frank Lampard

15. Alonso

16. Petr Cech

17. Jose Bosingwa

18. John Terry

19. Brentford

20. Portsmouth

.

Round 27

1. Which club signed Joe Cole from Chelsea in 2010?

2. Which England World Cup Winner also managed Chelsea?

3. Which fellow English club did Chelsea defeat in the Semi Finals of the 1971 Cup Winners Cup?

4. Which former Chelsea player was appointed Aston Villa assistant manager in 2016?

5. Which former English International managed Chelsea for just one game in 2009?

6. Which former player was appointed Chelsea manager in 1985?

7. Which French club did Salomon Kalou join when he left Chelsea in 2012?

8. Which Italian team did Chelsea beat in the Round of 16 on their way to the 2012 Champions League Final?

9. Which Chalsea legend was born on the island of Jersey?

10. Which manager guided Chelsea to the 2005 Premier League title?

11. Which manager was sacked by Chelsea in May 2004?

12. Which manager won the 2007 FA Cup with Chelsea?

13. Which manager won the Champions League with Chelsea in 2012?

14. In what year was Jon Neal appointed Chelsea manager?

15. What is the nationality of Chelsea's former manager Gianluca Vialli?

16. Which member of the 2016-2017 Chelsea Squad was Bosnian?

17. Which one of these Chelsea legends was Argentinian?

18. Which one of these Chelsea players also played for the Dutch national team?

19. Which one of these former players is Dutch?

20. Which player was signed from Marseille in 2004?

Answers

1. Liverpool

2. Geoff Hurst

3. Manchester City

4. Steve Clarke

5. Wilkins

6. John Hollins

7. Lille

8. Napoli

9. Graeme Le Saux

10. Mourinho

11. Ranieri

12. Mourinho

13. Di Matteo

14. 1981

15. Italian

16. Begovic

17. Hernan Crespo

18. Jimmy Floyd Hasselbaink

19. Dmitri Kharine

20. Didier Drogba

Round 28

1. Which player was on the shortlist for the 2004-2005 PFA Young Player of the Year?

2. Which player was signed by Chelsea in 200 from Atletico Madrid?

3. Which team did Chelsea beat 2-1 in the 2009 FA Cup Semi Final at Wembley?

4. Which trophy did Rafael Benitez win during his time at Chelsea?

5. Which was the only cup Ruud Gullit won as Chelsea manager?

6. Which was the only year of the 1990s in which Chelsea won the FA Cup?

7. Which Chelsea player is the youngest in history to received a red card in the Champions League?

8. Who at the time of joining Chelsea was the most expensive defender in English footballer?

9. Who at the time was the youngest ever captain in an FA Cup Final when he led Chelsea at Wembley?

10. Who beat Chelsea 4-0 in the 1994 FA Cup Final?

11. Who beat Chelsea in the 1967 "Cockney Cup Final"?

12. Who became the first player from his content to reach 100 goals in the Premier League in 2012?

13. Who began to manufacturer Chelsea kits in 2006?

14. Who began to sponsor Chelsea in 2006?

15. Who broke his leg in a challenge by Emmelyn Hughes in a 1966 League Cup tie?

16. Who broke his metatarsal in his first pre-season for Chelsea delaying his debut?

17. Who captained Chelsea to 4 Premier League titles?

18. Who captained Chelsea in the 1967 FA Cup final?

19. Who captained Chelsea in the 1994 FA Cup Final defeat to Manchester United?

20. Who captained Chelsea in their Champions League victory in 2012?

Answers

1. Arjen Robben

2. Jimmy Floyd Hasselbaink

3. Arsenal

4. Europa League

5. FA Cup

6. 1997

7. Celestine Babayaro

8. Graeme Le Saux

9. Ron Harris

10. Manchester United

11. Tottenham Hotspur

12. Didier Drogba

13. Adidas

14. Gulf Air

15. Peter Osgood

16. Arjen Robben

17. John Terry

18. Ron Harris

19. Dennis Wise

20. Frank Lampard

Round 29

1. Which English striker cost Chelsea £10 million?

2. Who cost Chelsea £16.3 million in 2008?

3. Who defeated Chelsea in the 2008 UEFA Champions League Final?

4. Who defeated Chelsea 3-0 in the 1915 FA Cup Final?

5. Who delayed making his debut to play in the 1960 Olympics?

6. Who did Ashley Cole join when he left Chelsea in 2014?

7. Who did Chelsea sing on a free Transfer in 1996?

8. Who did Chelsea beat 1-0 in the final of the 2000 FA Cup?

9. Who did Chelsea beat 1-0 n the 2007 FA Cup Final?

10. Who did Chelsea beat 1-0 on the 2010 FA Cup Final?

11. Who did Chelsea beat 2-0 in the 1998 League Cup Final?

12. Who did Chelsea beat 2-1 after extra time in the 2007 FA Cup Semi Finals?

13. Who did Chelsea beat 2-1 in the 2007 League Cup Final?

14. Who did Chelsea beat 2-1 in the FA Cup Semi Finals in 2000?

15. Who did Chelsea beat 2-1 on the 2012 FA Cup Final?

16. Who did Chelsea beat 3-0 at Highbury in the 1997 FA Cup Semi Final?

17. Who did Chelsea beat 3-2 on aggregate in the Semi Final of the 2012 Champions League?

18. Who did Chelsea beat 3-2 on aggregate to win the 1965 League Cup?

19. Who did Chelsea beat 5-1 in the 1970 FA Cup Semi Final?

20. Who did Chelsea beat 5-1 in the 2012 FA Cup Semi Finals?

Answers

1. Chris Sutton

2. Jose Bosingwa

3. Man Utd

4. Sheff Utd

5. Terry Venables

6. Roma

7. Gianluca Vialli

8. Aston Villa

9. Manchester United

10. Portsmouth

11. Middlesbrough

12. Blackburn

13. Arsenal

14. Newcastle United

15. Liverpool

16. Wimbledon

17. Barcelona

18. Leicester City

19. Watford

20. Spurs

Round 30

1. Who did Chelsea beat 5-2 on aggregate in the 2013 Europa League Semi Finals?

2. Who did Chelsea beat in a replay in the 1970 FA Cup Final?

3. Who did Chelsea beat in the 1971 Cup Winners Cup Final?

4. Who did Chelsea beat in the 2010 FA Cup Semi Final?

5. Who did Chelsea beat in the final of the 2013 Europa League?

6. Who did Chelsea defat in the 2013 Europa League final?

7. Who did Chelsea defeat 2-1 in the 2009 FA Cup Final?

8. Who did Chelsea defeat 2-1 in the 2012 FA Cup Final?

9. Who did Chelsea defeat 3-2 in the 2005 League Cup Final?

10. Who did Chelsea defeat in the 1998 UEFA Super Cup?

11. Who did Chelsea defeat in the final o the 1998 Cup Winners Cup?

12. Who did Chelsea defeat in the final of the 1997 FA Cup?

13. Who did Chelsea defeat in the final of the 2012 Champions League?

14. Who did Chelsea defeat in the Semi Finals on their way to winning the 1998 Cup Winners Cup?

15. Who did Chelsea pay £11 million for in 2001?

16. Who did Chelsea pip to the League Title by one point in the 2005-2006 season?

17. Who did Chelsea sign from Stoke in 2015?

18. Who did Chelsea sing in 2016 from Fiorentina?

19. Who did Chelsea top on Goal Difference to win the 1984 Second Division Title?

20. Who did Chelsea beat 2-1 in the final of the 1971 UEFA Cup Winners Cup?

21. Mason Mount wore which shirt number during the 2021/2022 season?

Answers

1. Basel

2. Leeds United

3. Real Madrid

4. Aston Villa

5. Benfica

6. Benfica

7. Everton

8. Liverpool

9. Liverpool

10. Real Madrid

11. Stuttgart

12. Middlesbrough

13. Bayern Munich

14. Vicenza

15. Frank Lampard

16. Manchester United

17. Begovic

18. Alonso

19. Sheffield Wednesday

20. Real Madrid

21. 19

# # #

Thank you for using this book, I hope you have enjoyed it.

If you have enjoyed the book, please leave a review wherever you bought it - this will help other Chelsea fans find and enjoy the book as much as you have!

# # #

Printed by Nevno Publishing, in the United Kingdom.

First printing, 2021.

Printed in Great Britain
by Amazon

78605195R00061